I0821673

FORMING OUR NATION

Making The Bill of Rights

by Wil Mara

LIGHTBOX
openlightbox.com

Go to **www.openlightbox.com** and enter this book's unique code.

ACCESS CODE

LBXY9359

Lightbox is an all-inclusive digital solution for the teaching and learning of curriculum topics in an original, groundbreaking way. Lightbox is based on National Curriculum Standards.

STANDARD FEATURES OF LIGHTBOX

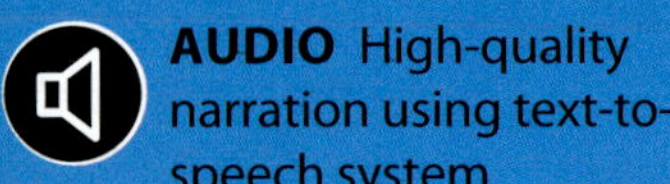
AUDIO High-quality narration using text-to-speech system

ACTIVITIES Printable PDFs that can be emailed and graded

SLIDESHOWS Pictorial overviews of key concepts

VIDEOS Embedded high-definition video clips

WEBLINKS Curated links to external, child-safe resources

TRANSPARENCIES Step-by-step layering of maps, diagrams, charts, and timelines

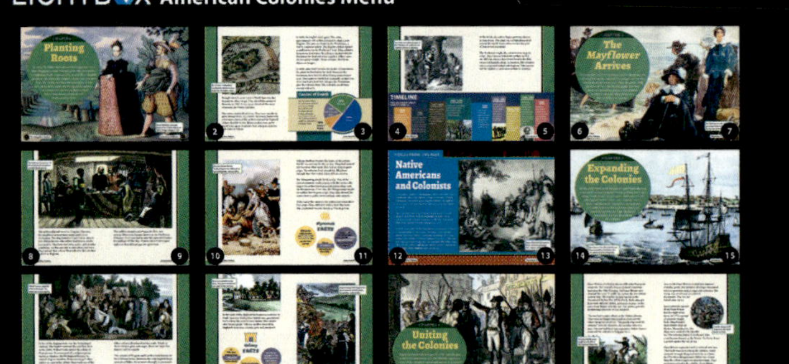

INTERACTIVE MAPS Interactive maps and aerial satellite imagery

QUIZZES Ten multiple choice questions that are automatically graded and emailed for teacher assessment

KEY WORDS Matching key concepts to their definitions

Making the Bill of Rights

Contents

CHAPTER 1

A New Government

The American Revolutionary War (1775–1783) was finally over. The United States was now an **independent** country. However, the U.S. government had many problems. For example, it could not collect taxes from the states. The government had no way to get the money it needed.

British soldiers surrendered to the American army in 1781. The war was officially over when a peace treaty was signed in 1783.

In 1787, many states sent **delegates** to a meeting in Philadelphia, Pennsylvania. Their job was to fix the problems with the government. The delegates had many debates. They decided to create a whole new type of government.

The delegates wrote the U.S. Constitution. This document explained that the new government would have three branches. The legislative branch would create laws. It was known as Congress. The executive branch would make sure people followed the laws. This branch would be led by the president. The judicial branch would decide whether laws followed the Constitution.

These three branches would make the government much stronger than it had been before. But not all of the delegates supported this idea. These delegates became known as Anti-Federalists. They said the Constitution did not give people enough rights. They also believed the government would have too much power over the states.

The Constitution was written in Independence Hall in Philadelphia.

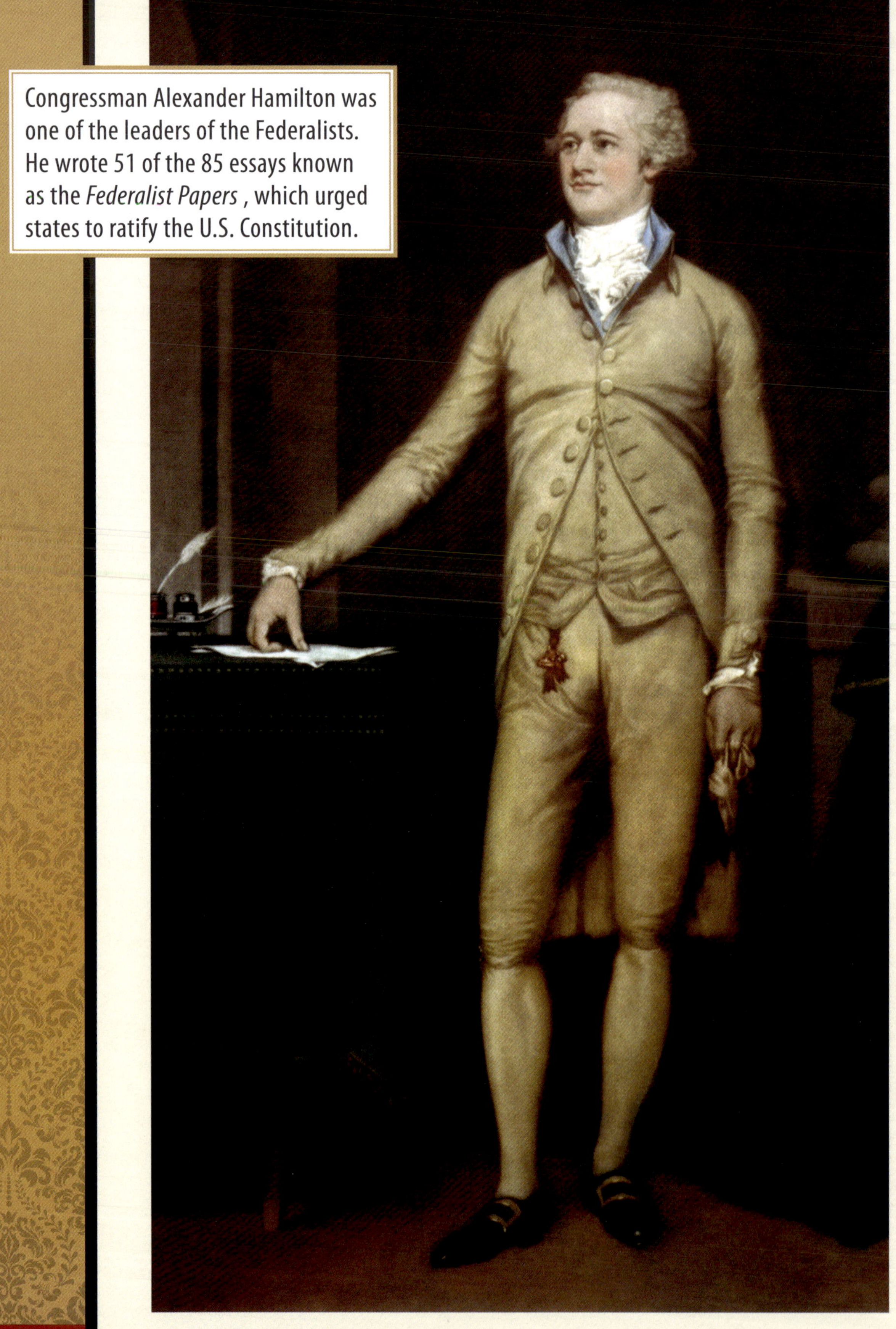

Congressman Alexander Hamilton was one of the leaders of the Federalists. He wrote 51 of the 85 essays known as the *Federalist Papers* , which urged states to ratify the U.S. Constitution.

Other delegates supported the Constitution. They were known as Federalists. These delegates believed the states could not handle issues that affected the whole country. For instance, a strong **federal** government would be better at dealing with foreign nations. The federal government could also solve disagreements between two or more states.

The Constitution was finished in September 1787. But the document would not be official until nine states **ratified** it. Delegates knew this process would take months. People on both sides of the debate began writing articles. They wanted other citizens to understand their views.

Constitution FACTS

The four-month meeting to write the Constitution was held in secret, with windows closed and blinds drawn.

Out of the 55 delegates at the meeting, only 39 signed the Constitution.

There are multiple misspellings on the original Constitution, including "Pensylvania," with only one "n."

Heated Debates

The Federalists and Anti-Federalists had many heated debates. James Madison was a Federalist. He wrote, "If men were angels, no government would be necessary." He meant that people did not always do the right thing. For this reason, a strong government was necessary.

Samuel Bryan was an Anti-Federalist. He wrote, "One general government . . . would not be so **competent** to attend to various local concerns." He was saying that many problems are specific to a certain area. The people living in that area should decide how to solve those problems. The federal government should not be involved.

Robert Yates was another Anti-Federalist. "The judicial power of the United States will lean strongly in favor of the general government," he wrote. Yates feared that the judicial branch would want to spread its power wider and wider.

James Madison later became the fourth president of the United States, serving from 1809 to 1817.

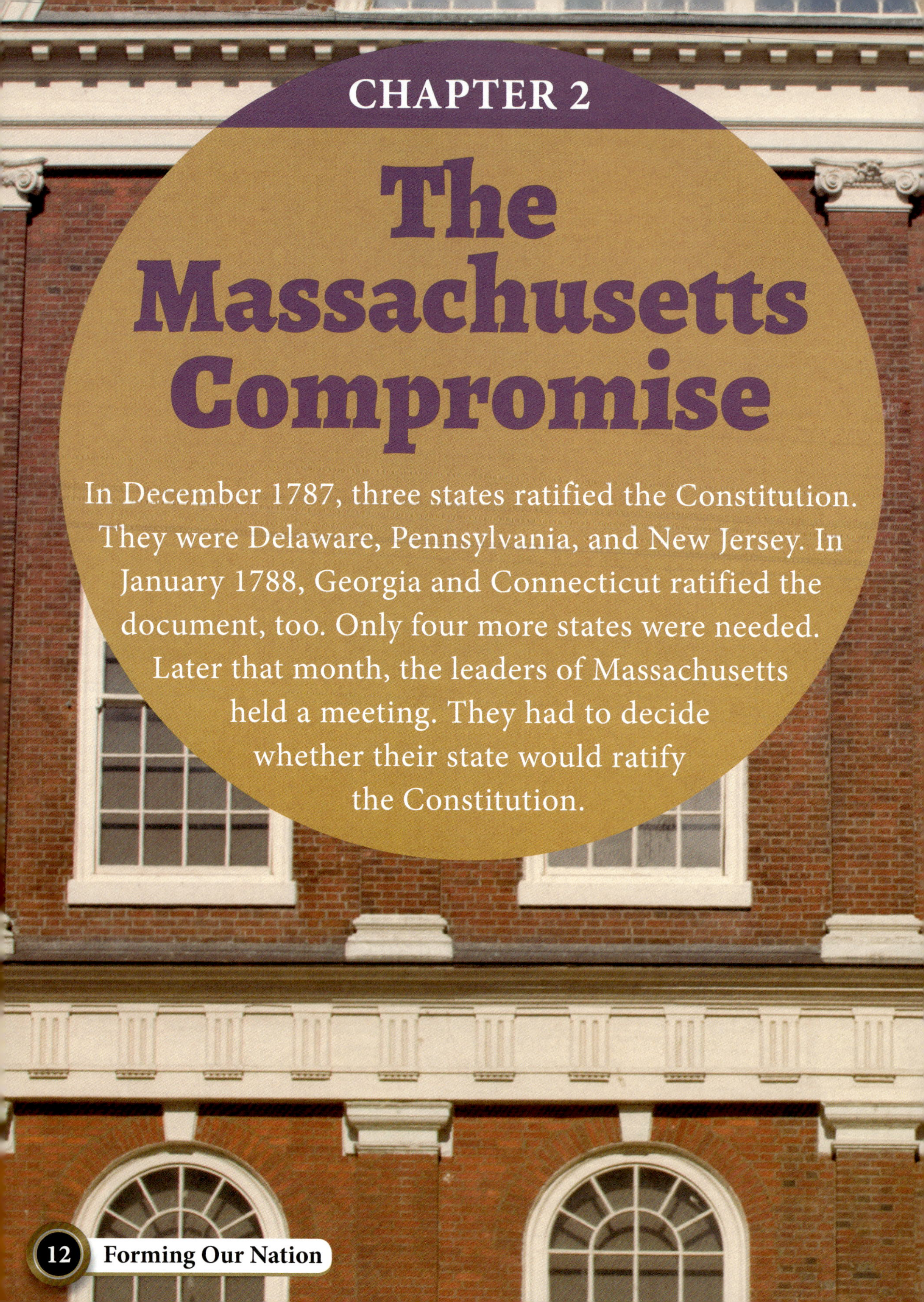

CHAPTER 2

The Massachusetts Compromise

In December 1787, three states ratified the Constitution. They were Delaware, Pennsylvania, and New Jersey. In January 1788, Georgia and Connecticut ratified the document, too. Only four more states were needed. Later that month, the leaders of Massachusetts held a meeting. They had to decide whether their state would ratify the Constitution.

Samuel Adams was a passionate politician and a leader of the Anti-Federalists. He later became lieutenant governor (1789–1793) and governor (1794–1797) of Massachusetts.

John Hancock was the governor of Massachusetts and worked to ratify the Constitution in his state.

Many Anti-Federalists were at the meeting. They included John Hancock and Samuel Adams. These men did not want to ratify the Constitution in its current form. Instead, they suggested a **compromise**. Massachusetts would agree to ratify the document. However, the state would suggest **amendments**. After all, the Constitution allowed changes to be made. The amendments would limit the federal government's power. They would also describe the rights of the people and of the states. The Anti-Federalists expected these amendments to be made as soon as the new federal government went to work.

TIMELINE

INSPIRATION FOR THE BILL OF RIGHTS

1770s

Many colonists were suspicious of a new government. They had been living—and suffering—under strict British rule.

June 1776

Virginia's Declaration of Rights, written by George Mason, is adopted. The declaration is later used as inspiration for the Declaration of Independence and the Bill of Rights.

March 1781

The first constitution of the United States, the Articles of Confederation, is ratified. The articles are quickly found to be lacking and many politicians begin calling for changes.

ARTICLES
OF
CONFEDERATION
AND
PERPETUAL UNION
BETWEEN THE
STATES
OF
NEW-HAMPSHIRE, MASSACHUSETTS-BAY, RHODE-ISLAND AND PROVIDENCE PLANTATIONS, CONNECTICUT, NEW-YORK, NEW-JERSEY, PENNSYL-

September 1786

The Annapolis Convention is held in Maryland to discuss issues with the Articles of Confederation. A larger meeting to create a new constitution is scheduled for the next year.

The vote in Massachusetts was close. But the state ratified the Constitution in February 1788. In other states, Anti-Federalist leaders took notice. They began asking for amendments, too.

In the spring of 1788, two more states ratified the Constitution. Only one more state was needed. In June 1788, New Hampshire became the ninth state. Similar to Massachusetts, it asked for amendments.

The Constitution was now official. But it was clear that many people wanted changes to the document. In March 1789, the new federal government met for the first time. Meanwhile, the Anti-Federalists were busy writing their amendments.

May–September 1787

The Constitutional Convention begins in May in Philadelphia. After much heated debate, the U.S. Constitution is signed in September. The document focuses on establishing an effective government and does not discuss the rights of citizens.

August 1787

During the Constitutional Convention, South Carolina delegate Charles Pinckney proposes a bill of rights. The bill is rejected. The topic comes up again in September and is rejected a second time.

December 1787

Having missed the Constitutional Convention while in Paris, Thomas Jefferson writes a letter to James Madison. Jefferson says the absence of a bill of rights is a major mistake.

July 1788

In the second to last *Federalist Papers* essay, author Alexander Hamilton argues against a bill of rights. He says it is not needed due to how the government and the Constitution were set up.

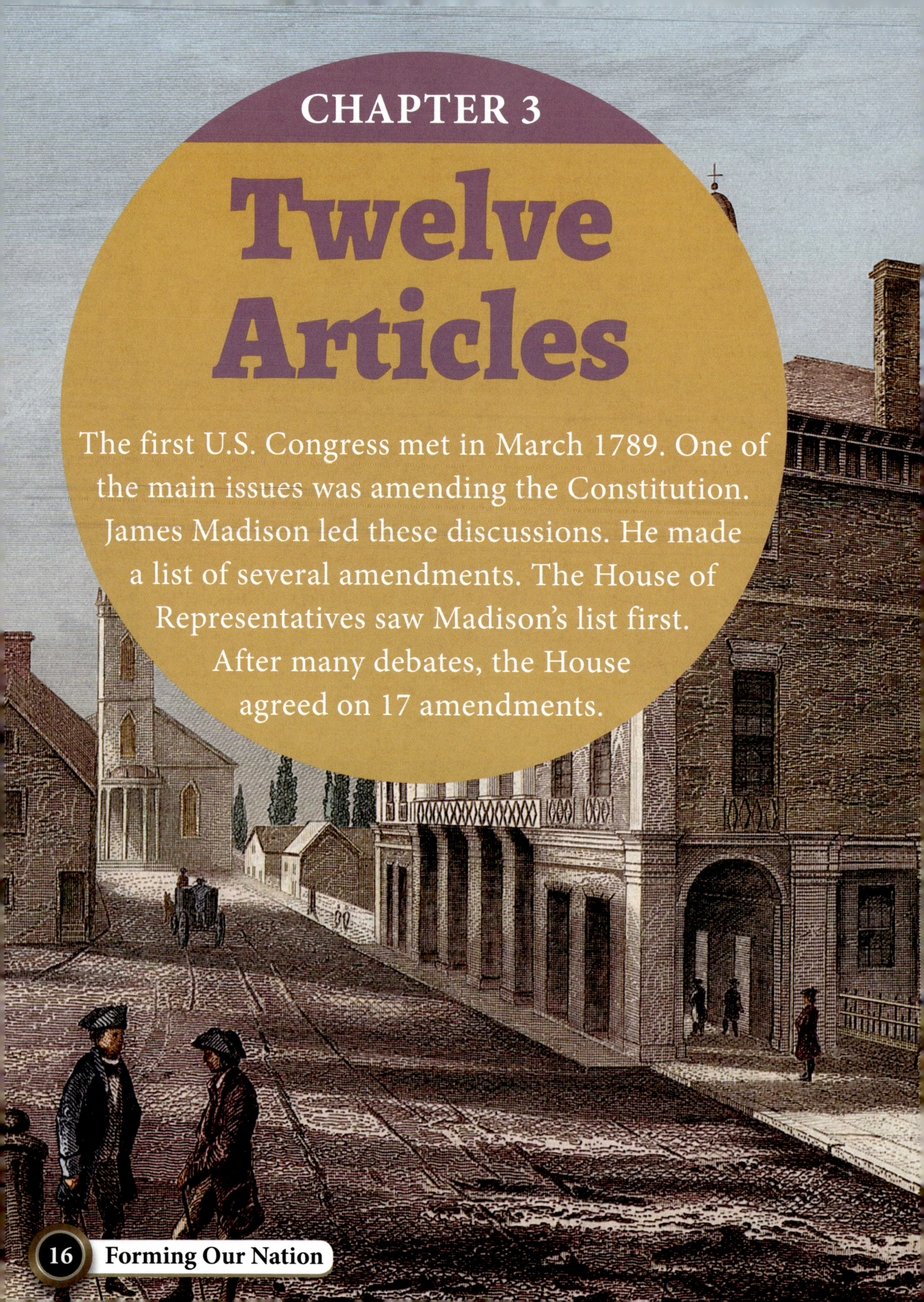

CHAPTER 3

Twelve Articles

The first U.S. Congress met in March 1789. One of the main issues was amending the Constitution. James Madison led these discussions. He made a list of several amendments. The House of Representatives saw Madison's list first. After many debates, the House agreed on 17 amendments.

The first Congress met in New York City, which was the U.S. capital from 1785 to 1790.

The freedom of press allowed newspapers to print articles that were critical of leaders.

The amendments were sent to the Senate in August 1789. The Senate had more debates, and the list went down to 12. Each of the suggested amendments was known as an article.

The first two articles had to do with Congress. The first explained how many representatives would make up Congress. The second described rules for changing representatives' pay.

The other 10 articles had to do with the rights of citizens. The third article gave citizens the freedom of speech, press, and religion. This meant the government could not stop people from speaking their minds. People could even speak out against the government. Also, the government could not stop people from writing their opinions. In addition, the government could not interfere with people's religion. It could not favor one religion over another.

Ratifying the Constitution

	State	Date Ratified
1	Delaware	December 7, 1787
2	Pennsylvania	December 12, 1787
3	New Jersey	December 18, 1787
4	Georgia	January 2, 1788
5	Connecticut	January 9, 1788
6	Massachusetts	February 6, 1788
7	Maryland	April 28, 1788
8	South Carolina	May 23, 1788
9	New Hampshire	June 21, 1788
10	Virginia	June 25, 1788
11	New York	July 26, 1788
12	North Carolina	November 21, 1789
13	Rhode Island	May 29, 1790

The right to form militias was important to many Anti-Federalists.

The fourth article gave people the right to own weapons. This right allowed people to defend themselves. It also let them organize **militias**. The fifth article said soldiers could not live in a citizen's house without permission. This had been a problem before the Revolutionary War.

The sixth article said government officials could not search a citizen's house without an order from a judge. The seventh said people do not have to **testify** against themselves during a trial. It also said a person cannot be tried twice for the same crime.

A fair public trial includes a jury of people who are not involved in the case in any way.

The eighth article gave people the right to a fair and speedy trial. The ninth article said if a person is being sued for more than $20, he or she also has a right to a **jury** trial. It also said the result of the trial could not be changed in a different court. The tenth article said criminals could not receive cruel punishments.

The eleventh article said people had rights that were not mentioned in the Constitution. However, the article did not explain what these rights were. The twelfth article said any rights not given to the federal government were automatically the rights of the people and the states.

Both houses of Congress approved these 12 articles in September 1789. But the articles were not official yet. For that to happen, three-fourths of the states would have to ratify them.

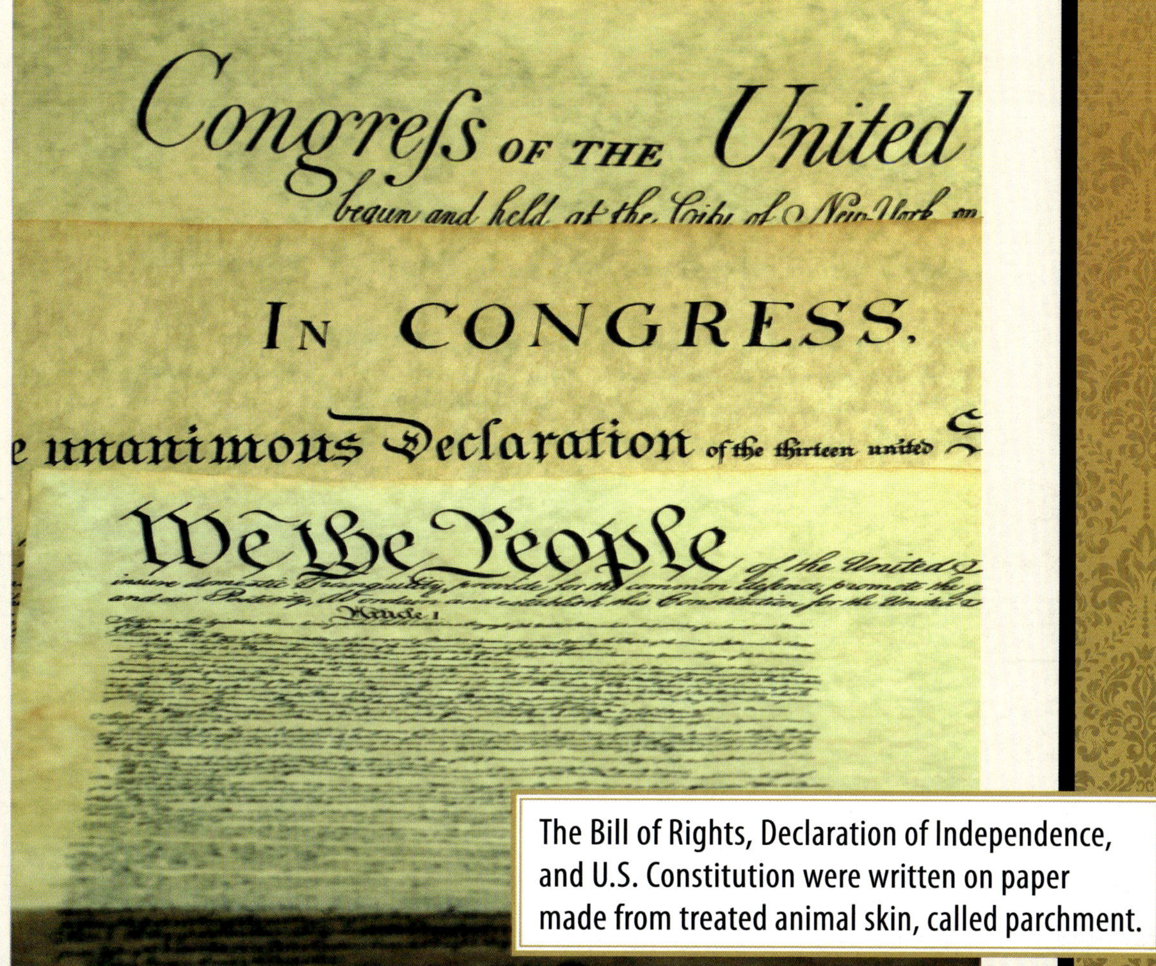

The Bill of Rights, Declaration of Independence, and U.S. Constitution were written on paper made from treated animal skin, called parchment.

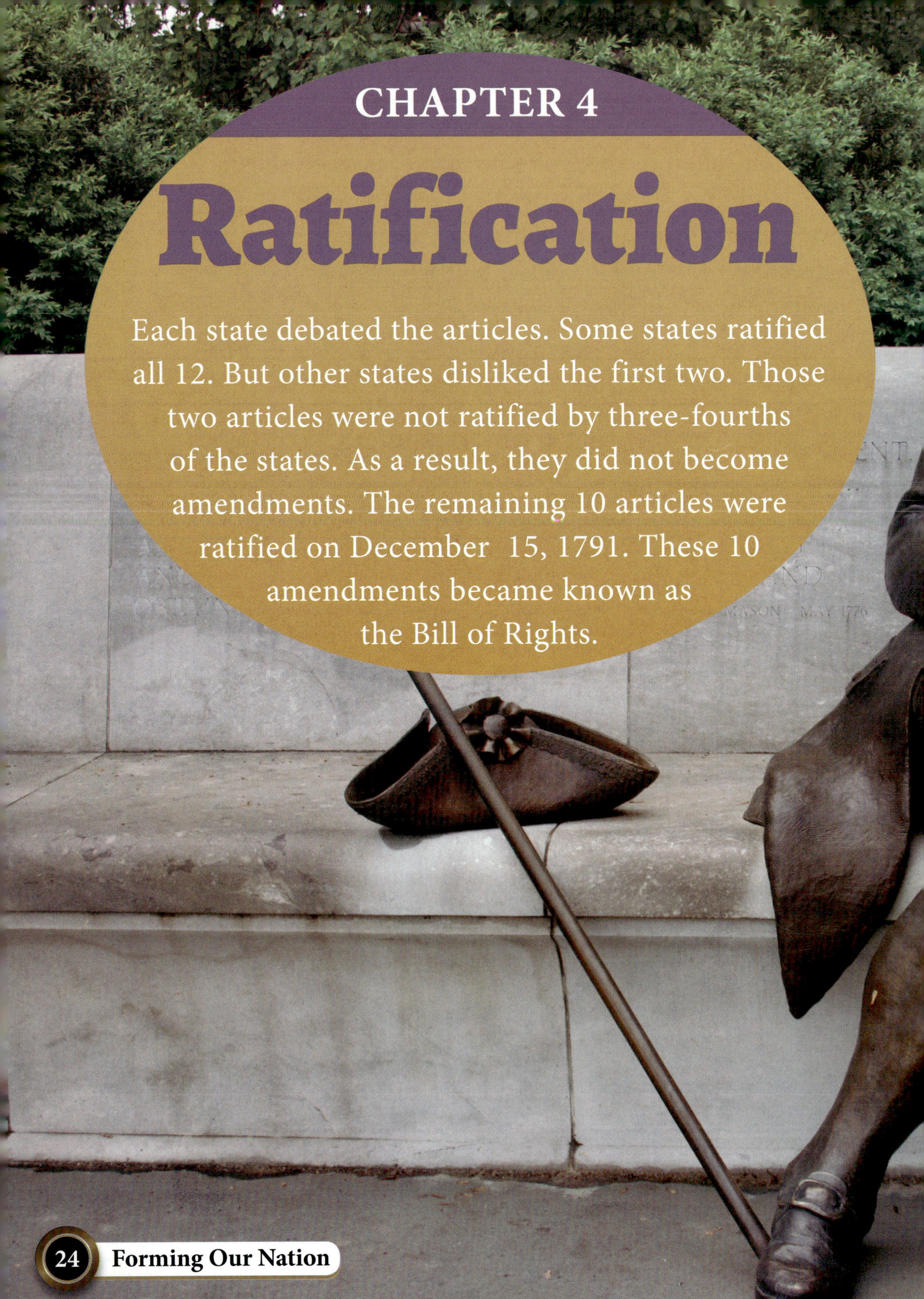

CHAPTER 4

Ratification

Each state debated the articles. Some states ratified all 12. But other states disliked the first two. Those two articles were not ratified by three-fourths of the states. As a result, they did not become amendments. The remaining 10 articles were ratified on December 15, 1791. These 10 amendments became known as the Bill of Rights.

George Mason, the author of Virginia's Declaration of Rights, believed a bill of rights should have been a part of the U.S. Constitution and strongly supported the ratification of the articles.

The first article was never ratified. However, the second article was finally ratified in 1992. That was 203 years after Congress first approved it!

The Thirteenth Amendment was signed by President Abraham Lincoln on February 1, 1865. It was ratified in December that year.

Many other amendments have been added over the years. One of the most important was the Thirteenth Amendment. It put an end to slavery in 1865. The Nineteenth Amendment was ratified in 1920. It gave women the right to vote.

The Constitution has been in effect for more than 225 years. One of the reasons for its success is that it can be changed. That was why the Bill of Rights became a part of the Constitution. People demanded a document that guaranteed their freedoms.

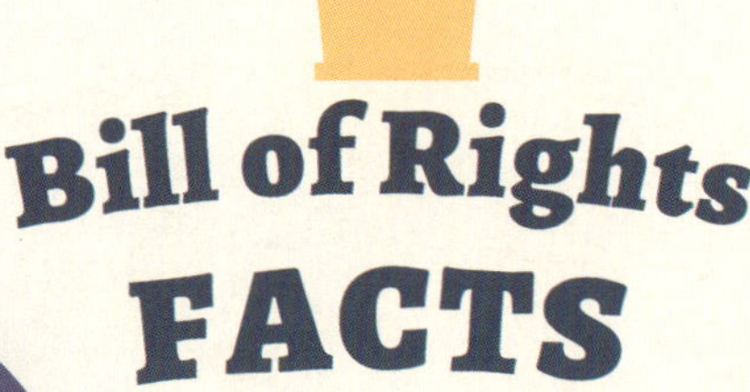

Bill of Rights FACTS

There is one spelling error in the Bill of Rights. "Defense" is spelled "defence," the British style, in the Sixth Amendment.

African Americans were not full citizens and not covered by the bill until 1868.

Copies of the Bill of Rights were given to each of the **13 states.** Five states—North Carolina, Georgia, Maryland, New York, and Pennsylvania—lost theirs.

MASSACHUSETTS
RHODE ISLAND
NEW YORK
CONNECTICUT
1
4
New York City
PENNSYLVANIA
NEW JERSEY
Atlantic Ocean
MARYLAND
DELAWARE
Washington, D.C.
2
3
VIRGINIA
N
SCALE
0 37 Miles
NORTH CAROLINA

Historical Documents

The founding and development of the United States was made official with several important documents. Multiple copies of each were made, but not all copies have survived. Many of these documents can still be viewed today.

New York Public Library

New York City, New York

The New York Public Library displays a copy of the Bill of Rights, which George Washington ordered to be made and sent to the states for review for ratification. It also shows a copy of the Declaration of Independence written by Thomas Jefferson.

National Archives

Washington, D.C.

The National Archives preserves and protects many original copies of historical documents, including the Declaration of Independence, U.S. Constitution, and Bill of Rights. They can be viewed in the Rotunda for the Charters of Freedom.

Library of Congress

Washington, D.C.

George Mason's 1776 Virginia Declaration of Rights served as inspiration for the Declaration of Independence and the Bill of Rights. It is held by the Library of Congress in the nation's capital.

Gilder Lehrman Institute of American History

New York City, New York

A private collection of early drafts of the U.S. Constitution, one with handwritten notes, is part of the Gilder Lehrman Institute. The Institute shares its collection with students through educational programs and resources.

Quiz

1 What are the three branches of government?

2 Which group of delegates did not support the idea of a strong central government?

3 What did Robert Yates fear?

4 Which 1776 document was used as inspiration for the Declaration of Independence and Bill of Rights?

5 Who led the 1789 discussions to amend the Constitution?

6 What did the original third article give citizens?

7 How many of the states had to ratify the articles?

8 Did the states ratify all 12 articles?

9 What did the 13th amendment do?

10 Which historical documents can be seen at the New York Public Library?

ANSWERS

1 Legislative, executive, and judicial **2** The Anti-Federalists **3** That the judicial branch would want to spread its power wider and wider. **4** Virginia's Declaration of Rights **5** James Madison **6** The freedom of speech, press, and religion **7** Three-fourths of them **8** No, only 10 **9** Put an end to slavery **10** Copies of the Bill of Rights and the Declaration of Independence

Key Words

amendments: official changes to a document

competent: able to do something

compromise: an agreement in which both sides give up something they want

delegates: people who speak on behalf of a larger group

federal: having to do with the top level of government

independent: able to make decisions without being controlled by another government

jury: a group of ordinary citizens who decide a court case

militias: military forces formed by ordinary people trained to fight

ratified: gave something official approval

testify: to speak in court

Index

LIGHTBOX

SUPPLEMENTARY RESOURCES

Click on the plus icon found in the bottom left corner of each spread to open additional teacher resources.

- Download and print the book's quizzes and activities
- Access curriculum correlations
- Explore additional web applications that enhance the Lightbox experience

LIGHTBOX DIGITAL TITLES

Packed full of integrated media

VIDEOS

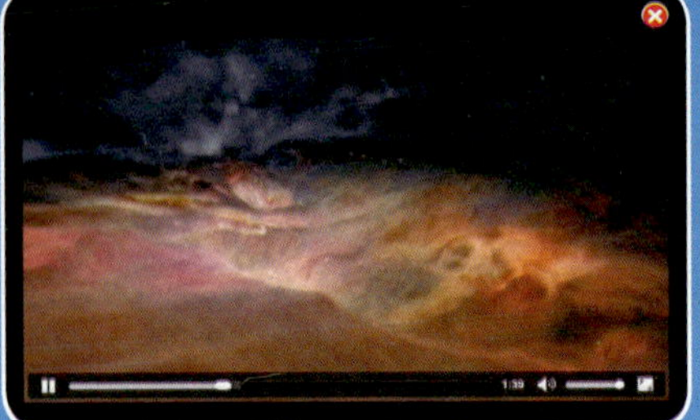

INTERACTIVE MAPS

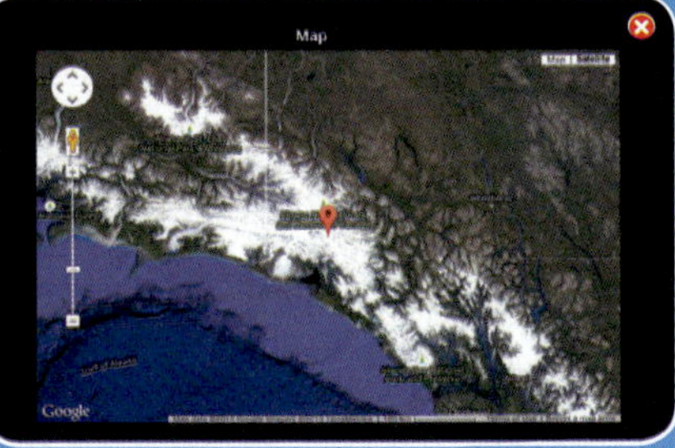

WEBLINKS

SLIDESHOWS

QUIZZES

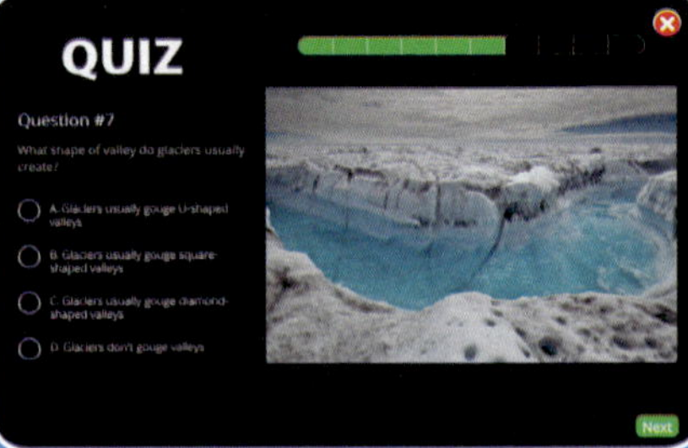

OPTIMIZED FOR

- ✓ TABLETS
- ✓ WHITEBOARDS
- ✓ COMPUTERS
- ✓ AND MUCH MORE!

Published by Smartbook Media Inc.
350 5th Avenue, 59th Floor New York, NY 10118
Website: www.openlightbox.com

First published by North Star Editions in 2018

Library of Congress Control Number: 2018936556

ISBN 978-1-5105-3793-4 (hardcover)
ISBN 978-1-5105-3794-1 (multi-user eBook)

Printed in Brainerd, Minnesota, United States
1 2 3 4 5 6 7 8 9 0 22 21 20 19 18

052018
111017

Project Coordinator Heather Kissock
Art Director Terry Paulhus

Photo Credits
Every reasonable effort has been made to trace ownership and to obtain permission to reprint copyright material. The publisher would be pleased to have any errors or omissions brought to its attention so that they may be corrected in subsequent printings.

The publisher acknowledges Getty Images and Alamy as its primary image suppliers for this title.